CHILDREN'S FAVORITE POEMS AND SONGS

Yankee Doodle

The Child's World®

Distributed by The Child's World®
1980 Lookout Drive • Mankato, MN 56003-1705
800-599-READ • www.childsworld.com

Acknowledgments
The Child's World®: Mary Berendes, Publishing Director
The Design Lab: Kathleen Petelinsek, Design and Page Production

Library of Congress Cataloging-in-Publication Data
Bangs, Edward, 1756–1818.
  Yankee Doodle / [written by Edward Bangs] ; illustrated by Robert Squier.
     p. cm.
  Summary: An illustrated version of the well-known song of the American
Revolution.
  ISBN 978-1-60253-534-3 (library bound : alk. paper)
  1. Children's songs, English—United States—Texts. 2. United States—
History—Revolution, 1775–1783—Songs and music. [1. Songs—United
States. 2. United States—History—Revolution, 1775-1783—Songs and
music.] I. Squier, Robert, ill. II. Title.
  PZ8.3.B223Yan 2010
  782.42–dc22 [E]   2010015204

Printed in the United States of America in Mankato, Minnesota.
July 2010
F11538

ILLUSTRATED BY ROBERT SQUIER

Yankee Doodle went to town

riding on a pony.

He stuck a feather in his cap
and called it "macaroni."

9

Yankee Doodle, keep it up,
Yankee Doodle dandy.

Mind the music and the step,
and with the girls be handy.

SONG ACTIVITY

Yankee Doodle went to town
(March in place.)

riding on a pony.
(Pretend to ride on a pony.)

He stuck a feather in his cap and called it "macaroni."
**(Pretend you are sticking a feather in your own
imaginary hat.)**

Yankee Doodle, keep it up,
Yankee Doodle dandy.
(March in place.)

Mind the music and the step,
and with the girls be handy.
(March in place and clap your hands.)

BENEFITS OF CHILDREN'S POEMS AND SONGS

Children's poems and songs are more than just a fun way to pass the time. They are a rich source of intellectual, emotional, and physical development for a young child. Here are some of their benefits:

❁ Learning the words and activities builds the child's self-confidence—"I can do it all by myself!"

❁ The repetitious movements build coordination and motor skills.

❁ The close physical interaction between adult and child reinforces both physical and emotional bonding.

❁ In a context of "fun," the child learns the art of listening in order to learn.

❁ Learning the words expands the child's vocabulary. He or she learns the names of objects and actions that are both familiar and new.

❁ Repeating the words helps develop the child's memory.

❁ Learning the words is an important step toward learning to read.

❁ Reciting the words gives the child a grasp of English grammar and how it works. This enhances the development of language skills.

❁ The rhythms and rhyming patterns sharpen listening skills and teach the child how poetry works. Eventually the child learns to put together his or her own simple rhyming words— "I made a poem!"

ABOUT THE ILLUSTRATOR

Robert Squier has been drawing ever since he could hold a crayon. Today, instead of using crayons, he uses pencils, paint, and the computer. Robert lives in New Hampshire with his wife.